Building Bridges

to the Heart of Discipleship

THREE INITIAL STEPS TO AN ENGAGING AND EVANGELIZING COMMUNITY

Leisa Anslinger and Stephanie Moore

D1515446

CATHOLIC
LIFE & FAITH

ACKNOWLEDGEMENTS

We wish to express our deep gratitude to the many parish and diocesan leaders who have shared their hopes, dreams, challenges and successes in building engaging communities over the past ten years. We are grateful for your witness as servant leaders who use your strengths to lead people to Christ through the Christian community. May we continue to learn and grow together.

DUPLICATION POLICY AND INFORMATION

BUILDING BRIDGES TO THE HEART OF DISCIPLESHIP

Table of Contents

INTRODUCTION

Are you ready to lead people to an encounter with Jesus Christ? Do you hope to form them as disciples and good stewards? Are you ready to build a parish community in which people grow as members of Christ's body, from which they are sent as missionary disciples? This is our hope as well. As partners with parish and diocesan leaders, we have seen parishes come alive with the love of God and grow as engaging and evangelizing communities.

It is this hope for strong parish communities that lead people to Christ and to Christian discipleship and mission that is the foundation of our ministry as authors, speakers and consultants and is the reason for developing the Bridges series. With over a twenty years' experience in leading workshops, retreats and in-service days, and following countless conversations with parish leaders who ask, "What do we do next?" or "How do we do this?" we have become convinced that very practical help is needed. That is why this series is being offered as a series of workbooks, presenting content, experience, and exercises in "do-able chunks" – just enough in each module to help parish leaders, step-by-step.

MAKING THE MOST OF THE MATERIALS

The Bridges series has been developed for all parish leaders (formal and informal).

- Read this book in the company of others – within your parish leadership group or small community.
- Use the included worksheets to aid your discussion while reading.
- Take time to read and discuss together using the worksheets indicated. This will insure that your study and discussions will bear fruit as you build a more engaging and evangelizing parish community.
- Access the online materials. This workbook includes access to learning videos and a guide, which includes additional reproducible worksheets. The videos cover much of the content found in this book, and have been created so that you may share what you are exploring with others, during parish meetings or leadership days.

LEARNING VIDEOS AND GUIDES

The accompanying learning videos and guides are found here at the link on page 58 of this book.

The materials include:

1. Preparatory discussion guide
2. Learning videos which present content and will guide your discussions
3. A participant guide that accompanies the video
4. A post-session worksheet
5. An optional introduction to engagement video

HOW TO USE THIS WORKBOOK

Consider any of the following options for using this workbook:

1. Read and explore the book (or use sections of the video) as part of regular parish meetings over a period of approximately 4 months. At the conclusion of this period, draw all who have explored the content (or representatives of each group) together for discussion and planning;

2. Form a committee that includes representatives of parish leadership and ministry groups to read and explore the content together. This committee will then share what they learn with the pastor and pastoral council and will suggest next steps for the parish;

3. Use the accompanying learning video resource with multiple groups or to guide a parish leadership day. The videos will prompt you to stop occasionally for discussion. We strongly encourage you to do so! Through your guided conversations you will surface things that are working within your current parish practice upon which you may build, and areas that need attention for the future.

Regardless of the option (or variation of options) used, your goal will be to develop an initial plan for building bridges as you form a more engaging and evangelizing community as a result of your reading and discussions with this book and its content.

Remember that this is the first of a series – there will be much more to explore, from which to plan for the future.

THE BRIDGES PROCESS: EXPLORE, SHARE AND PLAN WITH OTHERS

This workbook series is part of a larger initiative for pastoral leader development, which can be found at www.Bridge2Faith.net. You may contact us there for live events, participate in virtual courses, access previous session recordings, and learn about new resources as they become available. We hope you will go to the Bridges site often and stay in touch as we learn and grow together in order to build more engaging and evangelizing communities.

For whom has Bridges been developed? This series is for anyone who has influence in touching the lives of all within the parish and all who seek Christ:

- Those who have direct influence and accountability for shaping parish life, including the pastor, the staff, the Pastoral Council, and various committees/commissions (Stewardship, Finance, Evangelization, Faith Formation).

- All who form people in and teach our Catholic faith (children's catechists, RCIA team members, adult faith formation catechists and leaders).

- Those who lead ministries and organizations (Lectors, EMHC, Greeters, Hospitality, Choir, etc), as well as those who influence youth and young adult ministry.

- Any individual who is seeking ways to become more involved in shaping the direction of their parish would find this book helpful.

WHY BRIDGES?

We find the metaphor of a bridge helpful when thinking about the ways in which we can form engaging and evangelizing communities. There is nothing more precious than our relationship with Jesus Christ. And there is no one who can share our faith in quite the same way as each of us can. This is the foundation of Bridges: as members of Christ's body, parishes and people can have lasting impact on one another. We can touch those who are not rooted in a faith community, and we send one another out in mission, serving in our towns, cities, and world in Jesus' name. This gets to the heart of all we are and are called to be, as it leads us to the heart of Christ.

Why Bridges? Bridges lead us from here to there, across obstacles, through varying terrain, over tricky intersections. When we build bridges in our parishes and among our people, we stay focused on things that will lead to living faith as a disciple of Jesus Christ and a strong sense of mission. Through Bridges, we will help you develop this compelling vision for yourself as an individual and for your parish, and the skills to carry that vision out now and for the future.

Are you ready to form a more engaging and evangelizing community? Let's get started!

Why:
Parish Life Matters

Why: PARISH LIFE MATTERS

It is easy to look around us and see much that needs God's love and providence. People are impoverished, materially, emotionally, and spiritually; some are lonely, ill, touched by violence, left voiceless in the face of despair, grief, depression, and hurt. We know this. We see it, and sometimes live it, in our daily lives, in our families, neighborhoods, local towns and cities, and in our world. It is easy to look at all of this and feel that there is nothing we can do to change things. We feel small and powerless in the face of so much need.

It is in our human nature to long for closeness in relationship. We have been created with an inborn hunger for God and, often unconsciously, ache for that hunger to be fed. (CCC, 27) Not only this, we are created to be with and for one another, as our relationships have the potential to mirror the inner life of God, Father, Son and Holy Spirit. Yet many in our world, and in our personal lives, feel far from God and are at times separated from others in community. Being in community, in communion with others, is not within the worldview of many in today's culture. They find themselves longing for something, someone, yet they remain at a distance from Christ and the Church. We wonder what we can do to touch these people, many of whom are family members and friends, co-workers, classmates, and neighbors, with the love of Christ.

Each of us is created in God's image. We are born with the spark of divine life and light within us, and no matter how much darkness surrounds us, we are called to nurture that light and to bring it to the daily circumstances of our lives. Truly, the Holy Spirit nurtures the light when we allow it. And when we do so, we become collaborators with God in the ongoing task of creation. We can make a difference, and we must!

It may not be immediately apparent why we begin this book about evangelization, stewardship, and parish leadership in this manner, and yet this is exactly where we must begin if we are to fully grasp why this topic is of utmost importance. The world is not inherently "bad." The world most definitely needs the love of God, however, freely given through the members of Christ's Body, through our care and compassion, forgiveness and service, mercy, love, justice and peace. We are called to open our minds and hearts to the goodness of God and to bring that goodness to the people and situations that most need to be touched by it, as disciples of Jesus Christ and good stewards of all we are, have and will be.

DRAWN TO CHRIST THROUGH THE CHRISTIAN COMMUNITY

Our conviction is that when people are drawn into the Christian community they will be drawn deeply to Christ, to the heart of discipleship. Each of us has something to contribute to this work of God. As we grow within the community of faith, we are strengthened to go beyond ourselves, sharing the love of Christ through our service, sharing and witness. As parishes become more engaging, something wonderful begins to happen: not only are individuals more willing to reach out with God's love and the Good News of Jesus Christ as disciples and stewards, the parish community itself becomes evangelizing. The life of the parish leads those who are rooted within it to hear the message of Christ and take it to heart; those who arrive as guests or who are touched by the outreach of parishioners are led to an openness to God's love through the members of Christ's Body, the Church.

None of this happens by chance. In order to bring our communities to the fullness of this potential and these outcomes, we need to be intentional in our approach. We need to see ourselves as bridge builders to this amazing life as Christian disciples. When we build bridges within the parish and beyond it, we make connections between people and thereby link worship, faith and life to the heart of the individual. How do we do this? We believe there are very practical steps that will create these bridges that reach out, draw in, and transform our world in the process. When we intentionally focus on building these bridges, it transforms the parish in ways that brings new life and energy into the community of faith.

Why focus on building a strong parish community? We do not build up the parish for the parish's sake, but rather, to lead people to Christ and to form them as disciples, sending them out as people of mission. This is one of the most striking points of clarity in The Joy of the

Gospel: evangelization is to lead to missionary discipleship. This provides a clear vision for the parish community, a vision worthy of our time and attention, learning, discussion, planning and implementation. In fact, as Pope Francis presents this vision, he calls us to "devote the necessary effort to advancing along the path of a pastoral and missionary conversion which cannot leave things as they presently are. 'Mere administration' can no longer be enough. Throughout the world, let us be 'permanently in a state of mission.'"[1] "The parish is the presence of the Church in a given territory, an environment for hearing God's word, for growth in the Christian life, for dialogue, proclamation, charitable outreach, worship and celebration. In all its activities the parish encourages and trains its members to be evangelizers. It is a community of communities, a sanctuary where the thirsty come to drink in the midst of their journey, and a center of constant missionary outreach. We must admit, though, that the call to review and renew our parishes has not yet sufficed to bring them nearer to people, to make them environments of living community and participation, and to make them completely mission-oriented."[2]

Building up the parish is vital to the process of being in this state of mission, spreading the Good News of Jesus Christ by building bridges within the parish and beyond it. In this book, we will focus on the "pastoral conversion" of which Pope Francis speaks and which is necessary in order to "make them environments of living community and participation," making them "completely mission oriented."

As you have already seen, we will draw heavily on Sacred Scripture and Pope Francis' Apostolic Exhortation Evangelii Gaudium, The Joy of the Gospel, along with other Church documents and pastoral letters throughout this book. Our tone is intentionally informal, at times conversational. We hope you will think of us as partners in a dialogue that will lead to the development of thought and practice to strengthen your parish, forming a more engaging and evangelizing community of faith.

---

[1] Pope Francis. "Evangelii Gaudium." Vatican: The Holy See. Libreria Editrice Vaticana, 2013, 25.

[2] Ibid, 28

TAKE TIME TO EXPLORE TOGETHER. Use the worksheets below as your guide. The worksheet masters are available in the Guide, which is found via the link previously noted. Make a master copy of the worksheets to record your group's thoughts and insights for later use in planning. Use the space below to record additional insights or ideas for future reference.

What does it mean to evangelize? Why is this important? Simply stated, evangelization is sharing the Good News of Jesus Christ with others. Evangelization is at the core of who we are as disciples of Christ. Touched by the love of God through Jesus, we are compelled to enter into a life of conversion of mind, heart and life to the path of discipleship, through the power of the Holy Spirit. The nature of this ongoing process of becoming more like Christ means that each of us needs to be evangelized, and are called to evangelize, within and through the Christian community.

In the Joy of the Gospel, Pope Francis echoes and furthers the teaching of the Church since Vatican Council II in presenting three essential "moments" of evangelization:

1. Missionary activity directed toward nonbelievers and those who live in religious indifference;

2. Initial catechetical activity for those who choose the Gospel and for those who need to complete or modify their initiation;

3. Pastoral activity directed toward the Christian faithful of mature faith in the bosom of the Christian community. (See GDC, 49; EG, 14, EN, 7)

The Church exists to evangelize, and rightly so, for in doing this, we lead one another to bear the life of Christ in the world. "The fruits of evangelization are changed lives and a changed world – holiness and justice, spirituality and peace. The validity of our having accepted the Gospel does not only come from what we feel or what we know; it comes also from the way we serve others, especially the poorest, the most marginal, the most hurting, the most defenseless, and the least loved. An evangelization that stays inside ourselves is not an evangelization into the Good News of Jesus Christ." (GMD, 18)

It is this compelling mission that brings us together, to delve deeply into the ways in which we may build more engaging and evangelizing communities, sharing the love of Christ together, sending one another forth, as disciples and as people of mission.

CATHOLIC
LIFE & FAITH

Your Hopes and Dreams

BRIDGES
LEADERSHIP SERIES

This section draws on your experience as a beginning point. If you are participating in this module with others from your parish, take time to discuss the following focus questions together.

What are your hopes and dreams for your parish?
What would it be like to be part of your ideal faith community?

These sound like outlandish questions, and yet they are not intended to be. As you identify and name your vision for your parish, record it on the following page. You will share this with others as you begin this process together in building bridges to living faith.

- Record your thoughts on the left side of the table below.
- Record the highlights of their responses on the left side of the table below.

What are your hopes and dreams for your parish?	
What would it be like to be part of your ideal faith community?	

Describe what you imagine as experience of this ideal community would be like?	
What are the characteristics or elements that would be part of such an ideal parish?	

What common hopes, dreams, or characteristics emerge? Be prepared to share these conclusions.

CATHOLIC
LIFE & FAITH

The Joy of the Gospel

BRIDGES
LEADERSHIP SERIES

- Read this excerpt from "The joy of the Gospel."
- Underline or highlight words or phrases that strike you. Why is this important to you?
- Complete the questions at the end of the excerpt.

In the Joy of the Gospel, Pope Francis helps us to envision the evangelizing community, which we know in our hearts we desire. Let us be inspired by his wisdom:

"I invite all Christians, everywhere, at this very moment, to a renewed personal encounter with Jesus Christ, or at least an openness to letting him encounter them; I ask all of you to do this unfailingly each day."

Thanks solely to this encounter — or renewed encounter — with God's love, which blossoms into an enriching friendship, we are liberated from our narrowness and self-absorption. We become fully human when we become more than human, when we let God bring us beyond ourselves in order to attain the fullest truth of our being. Here we find the source and inspiration of all our efforts at evangelization. For if we have received the love, which restores meaning to our lives, how can we fail to share that love with others?

The Church, which "goes forth", is a community of missionary disciples who take the first step, who are involved and supportive, who bear fruit and rejoice.

An evangelizing community knows that the Lord has taken the initiative, he has loved us first (cf. 1 Jn 4:19), and therefore we can move forward, boldly take the initiative, go out to others, seek those who have fallen away, stand at the crossroads and welcome the outcast.

Such a community has an endless desire to show mercy, the fruit of its own experience of the power of the Father's infinite mercy.

"Let us try a little harder to take the first step and to become involved. Jesus washed the feet of his disciples. The Lord gets involved and he involves his own, as he kneels to wash their feet. He tells his disciples: "You will be blessed if you do this" (Jn 13:17).

An evangelizing community gets involved by word and deed in people's daily lives; it bridges distances, it is willing to abase itself if necessary, and it embraces human life, touching the suffering flesh of Christ in others. Evangelizers thus take on the "smell of the sheep" and the sheep are willing to hear their voice.

An evangelizing community is also supportive, standing by people at every step of the way, no matter how difficult or lengthy this may prove to be. It is familiar with patient expectation and apostolic endurance. Evangelization consists mostly of patience and disregard for constraints of time.

Faithful to the Lord's gift, it also bears fruit. An evangelizing community is always concerned with fruit, because the Lord wants her to be fruitful. It cares for the grain and does not grow impatient at the weeds. The sower, when he sees weeds sprouting among the grain does not grumble or overreact. He or she finds a way to let the word take flesh in a particular situation and bear fruits of new life, however imperfect or incomplete these may appear. The disciple is ready to put his or her whole life on the line, even to accepting martyrdom, in bearing witness to Jesus Christ, yet the goal is not to make enemies but to see God's word accepted and its capacity for liberation and renewal revealed.

Finally an evangelizing community is filled with joy; it knows how to rejoice always. It celebrates at every small victory, every step forward in the work of evangelization. Evangelization with joy becomes beauty in the liturgy, as part of our daily concern to spread goodness. The Church evangelizes and is herself evangelized through the beauty of the liturgy, which is both a celebration of the task of evangelization and the source of her renewed self-giving."

1. Who or what does this call us to be as a Church?

2. How might the excerpt influence the conversations of your group and the plans you may develop for your parish?

Who:
Servant Leaders as Bridge Builders

21

Who: SERVANT LEADERS AS BRIDGE BUILDERS

It takes strong leadership to build an engaging parish community. Leadership is not a word that comes up often in parishes, except when referring to the pastor and perhaps the staff. The paradox is that most would say that leadership is critical to driving the mission and vision of the parish, yet they limit leadership to the formal position of pastor and staff. From there, people look to bishops, cardinals and ultimately the Pope. And most certainly these people are leaders, critical ones to be sure! But leadership must continue to flow through every position of influence within the parish. The coordinators of ministries, pastoral council members, catechists, those involved in ministry and outreach, and even the parishioner who comes to Mass on Sunday, often do not see themselves as leaders, and yet they are. This is key: *every* person in the parish has influence in the life of the parish to one degree or another, overtly through particular roles within the parish, and subtly though the ways in which they interact with one another, building up the community of faith or failing to do so. The time has come for the word leadership to be clarified as it pertains to the faith community.

The concerning truth is that most people within the parish setting do not see themselves as leaders. Perhaps the reason for this is that is they adhere to the traditional view of leadership as it is experienced not only in parishes, but in most organizations. Even many business organizations are dramatically shifting away from the top-down hierarchical model of leadership. And while the Church is hierarchical in structure, the ways in which this structure is lived out can and should include all within the community, ordained and lay, through shared leadership in service and ministry.

Of course, our most important model of leadership is Jesus, who came among us "not to be served, but to serve". (Matthew 20:28) We have been baptized into Christ, priest, and prophet and king. As such, we are given the power and authority to live as members of Christ's Body as we build bridges back to God. In our priestly duty we are called to "consecrate the world itself to God" (*LG 34*) through our works, prayers, activities, and daily responsibilities. As prophets we are to announce Jesus Christ by life and word and be witnesses to "life springing forth from faith." (*LG* 35) As disciples, we share in Christ's kingship so that we too "might be constituted in royal freedom and that by true penance and a holy life [we] might conquer the reign of sin in [ourselves]" (*LG* 36). Christ's kingship is that of the servant. Therefore, we write and guide through a model of servant leadership. It is not surprising that Pope Francis, at the beginning of his pontificate, spoke of leadership in this way: "Let us never forget that authentic power is service."[3]

Robert Greenleaf, a former corporate businessman, is a primary proponent of the servant leadership model in the corporate setting. There is much that we can learn from these emerging business practices, since they get at the heart of how we can build strong parish leadership at all levels. In his book entitled "Servant Leadership," Greenleaf states, "A fresh critical look is being taken at the issues of power and authority, and people are beginning to learn, however haltingly, to relate to one another in less coercive and more creatively supportive ways. A new moral principle is emerging, which holds that the only authority deserving one's allegiance is that which is freely and knowingly granted by those led to the leader, in response to, and in proportion to, the clearly evident servant stature of the leader." He goes on to say, "To the extent that this principle prevails in the future, the only truly viable institutions will be those who are predominately servant led"[4] We will draw on Greenleaf and other sources of wisdom, experience and practice in leadership as we propose strategies for you and all who lead and serve within your parish.

Knowing that our mission is to give every individual the opportunity to grow closer in his or her relationship to Christ and the community, how does the leadership of the parish bridge those opportunities to each and every parishioner? Throughout this series, we will explore things you can do to lead people more intentionally into a life of discipleship through your roles and responsibilities and the ways you carry out these roles with others.

---

[3] "Homily of Pope Francis," March 19, 2013, Vatican.va.

[4] Greenleaf, R. K. (2002). *Servant leadership: A journey into the nature of legitimate power and greatness* (25th anniversary ed.). New York: Paulist Press, 24.

DISCIPLESHIP, STEWARDSHIP, EVANGELIZATION

As we continue, let us bring clarity to a few words we will use frequently, developing a common sense of three foundational and interrelated concepts:

Discipleship: Being a disciple is an ongoing process of following Jesus Christ with our lives. The path of discipleship is one of conversion, turning toward Christ, making conscious decisions to act as members of Christ's Body in the world. Pope Francis wisely begins The Joy of the Gospel by reminding us that openness to a daily encounter or renewed encounter with Jesus Christ is both a beginning and continuation of the life of discipleship.[5] Our lives are thus shaped by this relationship of encounter, expressed and developed within the faith community. When we encounter one another and those beyond the parish, we encounter Christ, leading us to more deeply embrace the life of discipleship to which we are called.

It will be helpful here to note that the rhythm of the liturgical year has the potential to shape our lives as disciples with open minds and hearts to ongoing conversion in Christ. Advent anticipation and hope lead to the Christmas celebration of the Incarnation; Ordinary Time in Winter bridges into Lent with its focus on turning toward Christ and living the Paschal Mystery; Easter's new life leads to Pentecost and back to Ordinary Time. While our life circumstances may lead to moments that seem out of sync with this liturgical rhythm, it is good for us to be aware that the Sundays and seasons, and of course the Eucharist, are at the heart of all we are and do, nourishing and shaping the life of discipleship.

Stewardship: The call to live as good stewards leads us to recognize that all we are, have and will be are God's. Christian disciples grow in willingness to embrace Christ's self-giving way, which is the way of the steward. The steward recognizes that all is gift, grows in gratitude for the many blessings given, and responds with generosity. Growing as a good steward calls us to the cultivation and sharing of our lives, faith, prayer, time and attention,

---

[5] Evangelii Gaudium, 3

talents and gifts, skills, knowledge and our material resources for the sake of others and the building up of the kingdom of God. We sometimes tease parishioners that we spend much time talking with people about two "scary" words for Catholics, evangelization and stewardship, and yet, when we do, fear dissipates, skepticism fades, and people's lives become richer with meaning and purpose.

Evangelization: Simply stated, having encountered Christ, we are called to share the Good News of the Gospel with others. While we are becoming more comfortable with the word "evangelization," many Catholics still get nervous when the topic arises. It is helpful to share that in our Catholic way of thinking, each of us needs to be evangelized, to be drawn more deeply to Christ, and that evangelization begins in our everyday interactions with others. This often calms the fear that "evangelization" will require people to stand on a street corner or knock on the doors of strangers. In the next section of this workbook, we will explore the need for evangelization and lay a foundation through which the people in our parishes may begin to see their role in sharing God's love with others through the faith community, their relationships with one another, and their care, concern and service for those in need.

When we read the Gospels and learn from the example of the early Christian communities found in the Acts of the Apostles and the New Testament letters, we are presented with a vision of who we are and who we are called to be as Christian people in community. We are called to live as missionary disciples, as people who evangelize and who grow as good stewards.

TAKE TIME TO EXPLORE TOGETHER. Use the worksheets below as your guide. The worksheet masters are available in the Guide, which is found via the link previously noted. Make a master copy of the worksheets to record your group's thoughts and insights for later use in planning. Use the space below to record additional insights or ideas for future reference.

Reflecting on Servant Leadership

Take time to reflect on our call to be servant leaders. Who drew you to service? Who will you invite to serve with you? Who or what first brought you to serve in a ministry or organization?

What has been the impact of this service on others? In your life?

Do you consider yourself a leader? Why or why not?

Who might you invite to serve? What talents or gifts do you perceive in this person? How might you call forth their gifts as a servant leader?

27

Building Bridges to the Heart of Discipleship

CATHOLIC
LIFE & FAITH

BRIDGES
LEADERSHIP SERIES

Becoming Bridge Builders: Consider who may join us, as builders of the bridges that will draw people to one another in community, and beyond themselves as people who care for others, sharing their love of God in service and mission.

Enlist others to build bridges with you as servant leaders: Help them see themselves as leaders, equip them with the tools they need by increasing understanding, building skills, and providing support every step of the way.

Servant leaders are servants first. They serve out of a deep sense of who they are as children of God, and they are committed to growing as people and as missionary disciples. People who understand themselves as servants and leaders recognize that we will contribute best to the mission and vision of the Church and of our local parish when we draw on the talents of each member, inviting every person to give of him or herself.

Build on a strong foundation: In order to build a bridge that will be strong yet responsive, we must build on a strong foundation.
- Share the content and conversations of this module with others who share leadership with you.
- Consider your parish or diocesan needs; build on what is already working; take time to plan and to carry out your plan.
- Learn through additional modules in this series, participate in virtual or live sessions as often as possible; form as many leaders as you are able, to build strong bridges that will endure in challenging times or periods of growth.

Consider your terrain: What bridges are most needed in your community at this time? We will propose three initial bridges next .
- Talk with others and discern what is already in place in order to strengthen a bridge, or what might be needed to repair or build a bridge that is in disrepair or currently absent from the life of your community.

What:
What People Seek

What: WHAT PEOPLE SEEK

Each of us is created in God's image. Most of us know this in our heads. We have been taught this from our childhood, and perhaps catch glimpses of it in special moments of prayer, insight, or experience in our interactions with others. Most of us, however, do not let this realization shape our daily lives. In fact, many of us wonder what difference this makes, if we think about it at all. Yet taking this to heart can have lasting impact in the way in which we live our lives. It causes us to reflect on who we are and who we are called to be. We begin this chapter with this realization because in doing so, we develop a spiritual grounding for stewardship and evangelization, as individuals and within our parishes.

Grasping that we are created in God's image not only helps us to appreciate our worth and that of the people around us, it also leads us to recognize the magnificence of God. "Unless people know the grandeur for which they are made," the U.S. Bishops say in their pastoral letter on evangelization, "they cannot reach fulfillment and their lives will be incomplete. Nor will they know that they are called into interpersonal union with God and with each other."[6]

In reflecting on who we are as people created in God's image, we begin to understand who we are called to be as people in our world: we are to bear God's image through the ways in which we live our lives. As Scripture scholar Dr. Art Zannoni has noted, we are to be the "transparency through whom God is seen."[7] Taking this realization deeply to heart, we may begin to grasp the potential we have for making a difference in the lives of the people around us, and we start to see our responsibility for reaching out to people as witnesses to the love of God through our relationships, caring and sharing.

Not only are we created in God's image, we are called to holiness. Speaking about this with parish leaders, we often initially see looks of puzzlement and sense a bit of anxiety in

---

[6] United States Conference of Catholic Bishops, "Go and Make Disciples". Washington, D.C., 2001, 31

[7] Zannoni, PhD. Arthur, The Bible Speaks on Stewardship, The Pastoral Center, 2011, 4

The Bridges Leadership Series

people's faces. "Holiness" is something we think about in relationship to the saints, not something to which many of us aspire. It is important for us to remember that God's grace goes before us, and in fact lies within us, as we consider this call to holiness, this call to live and grow in love. "They must therefore hold on to and perfect in their lives that sanctification which they have received from God."[8] How will we "hold on to and perfect" this holiness through which and in which we are created? We will do this best within a community of faith, in which each person recognizes his or her call to grow in love and to share God's love with others, as the transparency through whom God is seen. As a parishioner noted a few years ago, "It isn't as scary when we do this together!" We grow as God's good and holy people through and with others.

Created in God's image. Called to holiness. Let us connect these two realizations with our focus on strengthening the parish. When we, in our parishes and our relationships together as Christian people, recognize that every person is created in God's image, and when we together grow in love, through the grace of God, we will naturally reach out to others to share the Good News of Jesus Christ; we will turn more toward Christ and away from the selfish and self-centered ways that often shape our lives; we will grow in gratitude for all we are and have as gifts of God; we will learn together to share ourselves and these many gifts with others as good stewards. We will do all of this as a community, as people who, in the words of our bishops "are called into interpersonal union with God and with each other." We will be, as Pope Francis exhorts us to be, an evangelizing community.[9]

---

[8] Second Vatican Council. Lumen Gentium. Pastoral Constitution on the Church in the Modern World. 12 November, 1964. Ed. Flannery, O.P., Austin. Collegeville, MN: The Liturgical Press, 1992. 40.

[9] Evangelii Gaudium, 24

THE RELIGIOUS LANDSCAPE IN OUR TIME

We have already established that each of us needs to be evangelized and evangelizing. This is a running theme we will continue to explore, keeping in mind that "evangelization" is about ongoing conversion, transformation in Christ's life and love. With this in mind, let us turn our thoughts to the religious landscape in our time, focusing our attention on the people whom we may touch with the love of God. While we will specifically cite studies that focus on the United States, we know that similar patterns exist in varying degrees in other regions of the western world.

There is no doubt that things are changing in our surrounding culture where religion is concerned. Studies illustrate the shifts in the religious landscape, from a time in which the majority of people in the United States held a similar worldview, rooted in the faith tradition of their childhood, to our current reality in which greater numbers of people, particularly younger adults, are leaving the active practice of faith within a church or denomination, consider themselves "spiritual but not religious" or are simply unaffiliated.

We will briefly look at this dynamic from the evidence of the sociological studies momentarily. However, before we do, it is important to recognize that this section is not about statistics. It is about people's lives and our call to live as members of Christ's Body, sharing God's love with all. Chances are, you know someone who no longer regularly participates in Mass. It could be your spouse, child, or sibling. Or, you have seen the decline in participation in Mass or in the parish, and wonder what can be done to turn the tide. Maybe you yourself have moments in which you think about leaving, or perhaps you consider stepping away from the ministries in which you are involved, thinking you need a break in which to take stock of your life and the impact (or lack thereof) of belonging to your parish. It is easy to read the statistics about the changing religious landscape and think of the people described as "them" to our "us." And yet we know this was not Jesus' way. He embraced those who struggled with their lives and faith, and calls us to do the same. "We need to be reminded that we don't start with the religious question. We need to start with the human question. Jesus first did not demand conversion in the people he encountered. Rather he meets them at their level and says 'Let's have dinner.' Whatever religious experience or conversion that happens builds on that human encounter."[10]

It is easy to read the statistics and in our minds and hearts pass judgment on those who leave. We may do the same with those with whom we are closer in relationship, thinking (and perhaps even saying), "how very sad!" or "what a shame!" Throughout this section, we invite a different consideration of the current state of religious life in our culture. We hope that all who read and discuss the information will do so through the lens of our call to be Christian witnesses in the world, missionary disciples who are patient and show mercy, to emphasize Pope Francis' wisdom above. Rather than hearing about those who are unaffiliated and those who consider themselves "spiritual but not religious," and responding with a hearty "tsk, tsk" or becoming resigned to the decline and disinterest, thinking, "we may as well throw in the towel," we hope you will consider what follows through the perspective of a great evangelizing opportunity. We have good news to share: the love of God and salvation offered through Jesus Christ, the mercy and forgiveness of God, and the desire of the Church to welcome and embrace. While some pose difficult questions, arrive confused, and hold many misperceptions about the Church, we believe the appropriate approach is to build an engaging environment through which people may be drawn to Christ through the Christian community. By doing so, we will be ready to take the first step, meet them in the circumstances of their daily lives, and support them throughout their journey of life and faith.

With this desire firmly stated, let us become familiar with some of the current trends. If you know people who fit any of the descriptions that follow, picture them as you read what follows.

The Spiritual But Not Religious: Have you ever heard someone say, " I am Spiritual but Not Religious?" What does this mean to you? While those who use this phrase may mean a

---

[10] Reverend Ron Schmit, "Connections." October, 2014

variety of things by it, generally speaking, those who consider themselves spiritual but not religious have some sense of a spiritual dimension in their lives but do not see traditional, organized institutions as essential to their relationship with God. The data on the "SBNR" paints a slightly different picture than popular perceptions convey. It surprises many to find that the majority (65%) of the SBNR are religiously affiliated. 18% of Catholics identify themselves in this way. Slightly more than half of the spiritual but not religious are women. Approximately 7% of Americans consider themselves spiritual but not religious — a larger percentage of the US population than atheists, Jews, Muslims or Episcopalians. [11]

The Unaffiliated: The fastest growing group in relationship to faith and religion in the U.S. are the unaffiliated, now almost 30% of the American population. Nicknamed the "Nones" because they reply "none" to questions about church membership or affiliation on surveys, the numbers of unaffiliated people is on the rise across all age groups, particularly among young adults. For the most part the unaffiliated are not active seekers. 36% of Americans between 18-24 are unaffiliated; 34% of those between 25-33 are "nones." We will think more specifically about younger adults and what they seek in a few moments. While some of the unaffiliated describe themselves as having some spiritual desire or interest, most, particularly unaffiliated younger adults, have little interest in religion; it simply is not on their minds most of the time.[12]

The religious landscape in the U.S. is quite fluid. People move in and out of religious affiliation frequently, and for a variety of reasons. What is becoming clear in all of the current studies on religiosity in the United States, is that it is becoming more common for people to move from one denomination to another, often multiple times throughout the course of their lives. The most recent Pew Forum study indicates that Catholicism continues to decline among Catholics, although other studies show a slight uptick in the past five years. At best the

---

[11] Pew Forum on Religion and Public Life, "America's Changing Religious Landscape," May 12, 2015

[12] 2009 Newsweek Poll. See also Smith, Christian and Patricia Snell, Souls in Transition: The Religious and Spiritual Lives of Emerging Adults, New York: Oxford University Press, 2009, 295-296.

The Bridges Leadership Series

Catholic population is struggling to stay steady, and is most likely continuing to decline. [13] Among those who move from denomination to denomination, three-fourths say they did not feel their spiritual needs were being met in their previous congregation; some indicate they found a religion they liked more, or that they stopped believing in the teachings of their previous denomination; some say they had begun drifting away from their previous congregation long before they actually left. Others say they think of religious people as hypocritical, judgmental, or too focused on rules, power or money. Some who become unaffiliated do eventually return to a living life of faith, however younger adults are tending to stay away longer or to a greater degree than previous generations in their young adult years.[14]

Where does this leave us? The data does not only describe the groups of people who are part of the religious milieu at this time. From studies and personal experience, we can also gain glimpses into the dreams and desires of the people we hope to reach with the love of Jesus Christ. We will explore what the studies indicate that people (particularly younger adults) seek in the next section of this chapter. Let us pause here, however, for exploration and discussion on the above. Use the worksheet on page 42 to begin your conversation. Consider the first two questions now; leave the third question for discussion at the end of this section.

---

[13] Pew Forum on Religion and Public Life, "America's Changing Religious Landscape," Appendix C, May 12, 2015

[14] Ibid.

WHAT PEOPLE SEEK

With the brief look at our current religious landscape in mind, let us turn our attention to what people seek as they consider faith and/or belonging to a parish community. Certainly what follows is in some manner a broad generalization. Yet, with all of the evidence at hand, we may gain understanding into the needs that people hold in their hearts, and we may intentionally develop practices and strategies to address those needs through the faith community. What do people seek?

A spiritual dimension in their lives. As we have already mentioned, those who move from one denomination to another or those who become unaffiliated often say they did not feel their spiritual needs were met in their previous congregation. It is not surprising that people seek a spiritual dimension in their lives. Remember that inborn hunger for God? There is a seed planted within us that cries out for a relationship with our good and loving God, and no amount of cultural religious amnesia can completely erase this spiritual longing. Simply walk through a bookstore or browse online book listings and we quickly see evidence of this spiritual hunger in today's world. Hundreds of books are published each year on the topic, blogs are written and read, all pointing to this need for spiritual growth in our lives.

The indicators of the importance of meeting spiritual needs are not limited to the spiritual but not religious and the unaffiliated. Research on parishioner engagement indicates that meeting people's spiritual needs is foundational to engaging people in the faith community and in a relationship with Christ.[15] While the role of the parish in meeting people's spiritual needs makes great intellectual sense, this also touches at the heart of who we are as people drawn into community, into communion with God and one another. Surely the parish is a place in which people should find strength and guidance in their spiritual lives. Surely we would hope that every person is given what he or she needs to grow in and live out a faithful

---

[15] Winseman, Albert L., Growing an Engaged Church, New York, Gallup Press, 2006, 79ff

and fruitful relationship with God. Yet, when asked the question, "how are people's spiritual needs met here?" parish leaders often stumble, pause, and fall silent. We hope (and assume) people's spiritual needs are met in the celebration of the Mass and Catholic sacramental life, and surely they are at the center of our lives as Catholic Christians. Yet often, something is missing. Perhaps it is the spark of faith that has grown dim; at times a life challenge becomes a faith challenge and we are unsure to whom we may turn; sometimes there is a disconnection between Mass and the rest of life. In the words of David Kinnaman, president of the Barna group, in describing spirituality among young adults, "They see spirituality as connected to all of their life, not a compartment within their life. We need bridges between Monday-to-Friday and Sunday."[16]

A personal connection within the community. Reflect for just a moment on your relationship with people in your parish. Is there a person or group to whom you turn in moments of joy and sorrow? Does being rooted in the faith community make a difference in your life? Research helps us understand what our experience already tells us: having a personal connection to someone within the parish helps us to live our faith more deeply. What may be surprising is that the research actually indicates that belonging and living in faith share a causal relationship — belonging causes or encourages the outcomes we hope will deepen in people's lives, like daily prayer, forgiveness, encouragement, inviting others to the parish, giving of time and treasure in the parish and beyond it.- People seek a personal connection in the faith community; they know in their hearts the difference such a relationship will make.

In a large, international focus group, we are learning even more about this need for a personal connection. In 2013, Catholic Life and Faith opened its Spiritual Needs Survey. To date, over 4200 respondents have participated. The survey is still open for your participation. You may find information about the survey here: http://www.catholiclifeandfaith.net/spiritual-needs-survey. The survey was designed to create a means for exploring the question of spiritual needs. In working with parish leaders since the publication of the engagement research in 2006, many parishes developed initial plans to increase engagement, with

---

[16] Kinnaman, David, USA Today, 2010

increased belonging and the outcomes they hoped to foster. Following the initial plans, however, parish leaders often return to the question of spiritual needs. What are people's spiritual needs? How can we meet those needs within the parish? Isn't Mass enough to meet the needs any of us will have throughout our lives?

We are still learning from the survey responses, and leave it open so that parishes or dioceses may participate and learn from their own local responses. It is important to recognize that this is not a random statistical survey, but rather, it can be considered a large focus group. People agree to participation; most hear about it at Sunday Mass, so are present at least some of the time. The responses are providing striking evidence of the relationship between spiritual needs and personal connection, which we believe is crucial in our discussions here.

Three survey questions highlight this relationship:

What helps you grow spiritually? *	What helps you find meaning or purpose in life?	For faith that needs strengthening, you would participate in:
1. Participation in Mass 2. Daily prayer 3. Belonging to my parish 4. Good friends who share faith with me	1. Family 2. Faith 3. Friends	1. A faith mentor 2. Parish gatherings to explore spiritual life

*Responses of younger adults, ages 18-24, include the same four but in a different order: 1.) Mass; 2) Good friends; 3) Daily prayer; 4) Belonging to my parish

These responses highlight the connection between spiritual needs and growth and personal relationships among people within the faith community. No doubt there are things we can do to directly influence the way people grow in their spiritual lives. Some of the survey responses point to things such as small groups, book clubs, etc. What is encouraging is the correlation between the responses on the survey and the larger sociological studies such as those by Gallup, the Pew Forum, and Dr. Christian Smith who all point to the importance of the faith community in people's lives. There is much more to learn as we delve into the insights shared in the survey, and hope you will consider offering it to your members as a way to hear from them and to enhance what we are learning for the future. One big take-away from the survey is the importance of helping people to connect with one another within the faith community.

The opportunity to contribute to mission and to make an impact. We are hard-wired to give. Giving unleashes our potential to make a contribution to the world, and in doing so, we find meaning and purpose in our lives and experience physical and emotional health benefits. In our parishes, it seems natural to invite people to give of their time, financial resources and talents, since doing so is essential to fulfilling the mission of Christ and the Church, giving of ourselves, sacrificially, as members of Christ's Body. Offering people opportunities to give, however, often seems extraneous rather than integral to the rhythm of parish life as a response to the call of discipleship. Seasonal food and/or clothing drives are a good example of common parish practices that require the commitment of parishioners to organize and carry out for the sake of others. How we communicate about these opportunities, and the ways in which they fit in a wider scheme of mission, service, and outreach should be regularly examined and adjusted for the greatest impact upon the receivers as well as the givers.

Linking Christ's call to share and to serve with the impact on both the giver and receiver is crucial to engaging people in the parish community as disciples, especially younger adults. 85% of Millennials say they are motivated to give by a compelling mission or cause.[17] Answering the call to mission engages people in the parish, often by starting with small "micro-

---

[17] Millennial Impact Report, 2013.

volunteering" experiences. These one-off opportunities to give of time or talent often lead to a greater commitment to be involved, especially when participants recognize the impact of their giving.

What do people seek? While there are many other things on which we could focus, social science and the experience of pastoral leaders suggest these three things provide ample opportunity for initial attention and growth: be aware of people's need for a spiritual dimension in their lives; help people to become connected with one another; and give them a way to live in mission and find meaning in their giving.

This brings us back full-circle, but with additional insight into the vital role of the parish in bringing people to a deep, lived relationship with Jesus Christ. Those of us who are already rooted in the faith community may underestimate the impact of an engaging parish in the lives of the people around us. Yet everything that we have considered above points to this crucial matter, which is foundational to all that follows in this book: parish life matters. Throughout the Bridges process, we will propose specific steps servant leaders can take to "review and renew" their parish, to make it an environment of "living community and participation,"[18] leading them to live the mission of Christ in the world.

---

[18] Evangelii Gaudium, 28

TAKE TIME TO EXPLORE TOGETHER. Use the worksheets below as your guide. The worksheet masters are available in the Guide, which is found via the link previously noted. Make a master copy of the worksheets to record your group's thoughts and insights for later use in planning. Use the space below to record additional insights or ideas for future reference.

From a personal perspective
- What is your personal experience? Do you know someone who considers him or herself Spiritual But Not Religious or who is now unaffiliated? What do you learn from them?

From a communal perspective
- Has your parish experienced declining participation in Mass or involvement in ministries and organizations? To what so you attribute your parish's experience of growth, stability or decline?

From the Church perspective
- How may the things you recognized above be influenced by Pope Francis' description of the evangelizing community and its impact?

How:
Three Initial Bridges

The Bridges Leadership Series

How: THREE INITIAL BRIDGES

The three initial bridges we propose here are directly tied to all we have considered previously in this workbook: our call to discipleship and evangelization, the current religious landscape, the hopes and desires of people, especially young adults, and the importance of a strong parish community in which to live and grow in faith. Later modules explore many aspects of the process of building such an engaged and evangelizing community and equip leaders for it. These three initial bridges are integral to the rest, and are good starting points for conversations among leaders and the plans of action that result from those conversations. As we begin, let us briefly look at two preliminary considerations:

Build on a strong foundation: In order to build a bridge that will be strong yet responsive, we must build on a strong foundation. Share the content and conversations of this module with others who share leadership with you. Consider your parish or diocesan needs; build on what is already working; take time to plan and to carry out your plan. Learn through additional modules in this series, participate in virtual or live sessions as often as possible; form as many leaders as you are able, to build strong bridges that will endure in challenging times or periods of growth.

Consider your terrain: What bridges are most needed in your community at this time? We will propose three initial bridges below. Talk with others and discern what is already in place in order to strengthen a bridge, or what might be needed to repair or build a bridge that is in disrepair or currently absent from the life of your community.

BRIDGE #1: WELCOME

St. Benedict, in his rule for his community, wrote, "Any guest who happens to arrive at the monastery should be received just as we would receive Christ himself, because he promised that on the last day he will say I was a stranger and you welcomed me." (Rule of St. Benedict, Chapter 53) His direction touches on the heart of Christian hospitality. We do not know the pain or emptiness a person may carry with him or her when arriving at the parish; we cannot glimpse from the outside the desire a person may have within her or his heart; we only know that every person is valued as a child of God and therefore must be welcome among us. Pope Francis speaks to the need for genuine hospitality: "Instead of being just a church that welcomes and receives by keeping doors open, let us also try to be a church that finds new roads, that is able to step outside itself and go to those who do not attend Mass, to those who have quit or are indifferent. The ones who quit sometimes do it for reasons that, if properly understood and assessed, can lead to a return. But that takes audacity and courage." (Pope Francis, interview published in American Magazine, September 19, 2013)

Audacious and courageous hospitality! That is the sort of welcome we must build in our communities in order for people to be drawn more deeply to Christ. Let us be honest, audacity and courage are needed at both sides of this bridge. Those who reach out must take courage, knowing that they may be rejected or met with suspicion. Those who receive an offer of welcome may also need courage, to set aside fear, preconceived perceptions, or previous negative experiences. There is risk on both sides of this bridge. In offering or receiving a genuine welcome, we often feel vulnerable. Yet such real and open-hearted hospitality changes the way in which we experience the mystery of God's love in the Eucharist and sacraments. This desire to be-with echoes and carries with it a vision of Christ's desire to live and be with us.

This genuine welcome is as much about who we are as what we do. This is about more than smiling at people as they arrive for Sunday Mass (although that is a good place to start

45

and an important ministry of hospitality). True hospitality takes place when people are invited to be themselves and to meet the love of Christ in the process.

At times, our call to be welcoming seems at odds with Church teaching. We may worry we might send a mixed message about who may or may not receive Holy Communion. We might be concerned that various "hot topics" will emerge that could undermine the sense of community we hope to build. These topics are beyond the scope of this module. However, let us offer a few thoughts for your later discussions. Welcoming people into the community is not the same as inviting them to the Eucharistic table. What practices might you put in place in order to invite the greatest participation of all while not overstepping what we believe and teach about Communion and being in communion?

Consider how you are forming your community to respond appropriately to questions that arise among friends and family. Do they know to whom they may bring questions or the people who ask them? Is there regular opportunity for well-informed and respectful discussion among youth and adults? Our experience helps us understand that welcoming people respectfully and inviting their participation in ways appropriate for them within the boundaries of Catholic teaching is a deeply meaningful way of evangelizing them and their families, leading people to relationship with God which shapes their lives.

Invite people into the family. Inviting a guest to the parish is like inviting a friend to a family gathering. When we bring a friend with us to a family gathering, we do not introduce the friend to everyone and leave them to their own devices. Often, we tell the friend stories so they will understand family traditions; we draw them into conversation with family members, and share the impact special people within the family have had on our lives. Likewise, when we bring people to the parish, it is reassuring for them to know that we will not leave them alone, or that we will be nearby. Coming into a parish function in which everyone seems to know everyone else is disconcerting. The visitor my feel neglected or left out, negating any hope that the friend may return on his or her own!

Building the bridge of welcoming is most effectively accomplished by building a strong community in which people have a deep sense of belonging within the parish. Build on those who are already engaged in the community. The goal is to know that when someone arrives at the parish, he or she is likely to meet many people who call the parish "home" before encountering the one, fussy person who always makes sure everyone knows just how bad things are there! The bridge of welcome opens the door to a relationship with Christ that changes the life of the individual and the life of the parish.

BRIDGE #2: FRIENDSHIP

"The two disciples heard him (John the Baptist) say this, and they followed Jesus. When Jesus turned and saw them following, he said to them, "What are you looking for?" They said to him, "Rabbi"..."where are you staying?" He said to them, "Come and see." (John 1:35-43)

We have already established the need to connect people with one another, building bridges to faith-filled relationships. We cannot force friendship, of course, but we may certainly offer many opportunities for people to get to know one another, to share their lives and faith with each other, and to build relationships that will grow over time. When the first disciples approached Jesus, he did not offer them a program, nor did he begin teaching them all that he was about right from the start. Rather, he drew them into relationship with him. He invited them to come and see, to get to know him. Sometimes people come to us wanting to know about Jesus or the Church. There is a time for teaching, and a need for it as well. Most people, however, first need to be in relationship with others in the community, and through those relationships, they grow in a desire to know Christ and the Church. As they grow in friendship within the community, they will be drawn into a relationship with Jesus, and to live their faith more deeply in all aspects of their lives.

Consider the ways in which you may invite people to become acquainted: through youth, younger adults, older adults; through small groups that focus on particular life circumstances, areas of interest, or for prayer or learning; in mentoring or reverse-mentoring opportunities in which people meet one -on -one for prayer, faith sharing, and conversation. Once you begin to think about this bridge, opportunities to draw people into friendship within the community are sure to emerge. The bridge of friendship will have lasting impact within the parish and beyond it.

BRIDGE #3: SHARING

"In this period of crisis today, it is important not to turn in on ourselves, burying our own talent, our spiritual, intellectual, and material riches, everything that The Lord has given us; but rather to open ourselves, to be supportive, to be attentive to others. Set your stakes on great ideals, the ideals that enlarge the heart, the ideals of service that make your talents fruitful. Life is not given to us to be jealously guarded for ourselves, but is given to us so that we may give it in turn." (Pope Francis, April 24, 2013)

We know that people to be encouraged and invited to give of themselves, and the desire of people to grasp the impact their giving may have on those who receive. And we have tied this giving to the mission of Christ and the Church. We recall Jesus' commands to wash one another's feet and to serve the least of our brothers and sisters. Parishes that intentionally develop a strong sense of discipleship and mission find that doing so enlivens people, provides opportunities to engage those who might otherwise remain on the periphery of parish life, and encourages growth in shared leadership.

There are two ways in which we may encourage and experience sharing: sharing of self and resources in service of others, and sharing of our relationship with Christ. Think of the community as a series of concentric circles. Encourage those who are already deeply involved and engaged to reach out to those they know, or those of whom they become aware; those who are drawn in will then be encouraged to reach out to those just beyond themselves. The bridges move from the "inside" circles to the "outer" ones, breaking down any walls, silos, or cliques in the process. Pay particular attention to the ways in which already-connected parishioners may be encouraged to invite, welcome, witness and lead others to become rooted in the faith community and to build bridges beyond it.

"The Lord made bridges…Christians who are afraid to build bridges and prefer to build walls are Christians who are not sure of their faith, not sure of Jesus Christ…Build bridges and move forward." (Pope Francis, May 8, 2013)

TAKE TIME TO EXPLORE TOGETHER. Use the worksheets below as your guide. The worksheet masters are available in the Guide, which is found via the link previously noted. Make a master copy of the worksheets to record your group's thoughts and insights for later use in planning. Use the space below to record additional insights or ideas for future reference.

Building Bridges: Next Steps

CATHOLIC
LIFE & FAITH

BRIDGES
LEADERSHIP SERIES

- Use the table below to discover attributes of bridges that already exist within your parish.
- Record in column two your dreams for growth in bridge building in the coming year.
- In columns three and four, begin to develop your plan for these initial steps in building an engaging and evangelizing parish by building bridges as servant leaders.

	Discover (Be attentive) What we do best? Build on current engagement	Dream (Be intelligent) What might be? What is your vision?	Discern (Be realistic) What should be? How to begin and with whom?	Do (Be responsible) What will be? Plan to build the dream.
WELCOME				
FRIEND-Ship				
SHARING				

Your Next Steps

The Bridges Leadership Series

YOUR NEXT STEPS

As we conclude this first module of the Bridges series, identify your immediate next steps:

- Schedule a meeting. If multiple groups are discussing this content simultaneously, schedule a meeting for groups or their representatives to compile insights, hopes, and concerns;

- Develop an initial plan to draw others into this vision of servant leaders as builders of bridges. Consider holding a parish leadership day as part of your initial plan.

- Discuss ways in which your parish may build bridges to the heart of discipleship, beginning with the three initial bridges of welcome, friendship and sharing;

- Consider which elements of the Bridges path are appropriate for your parish. See description of the path and the resources to help you on this journey, beginning on page 55.

- Determine what group(s) will continue with the Bridges series module 2 on Creating a Parish Covenant.

- Continue to explore through the web series Bridges Now, and consider a live or virtual session for your leaders with one of the Catholic Life and Faith team. Contact us via the link on the Bridges website: www.Bridge2Faith.net.

- Please take our brief survey about this workbook and the Bridges Leadership Series. Your feedback, experience, and insights will enhance the ways we may partner with leaders like you in the future. The survey is here: https://www.surveymonkey.com/s/BridgesBook

You have taken a big step toward an engaging and evangelizing community through the discussions and plans you have made as you have progressed through this workbook! Just as we are never "finished" disciples, so too, our communities are never "finished." As soon as we begin to think that we are, we either continue to build and to grow, or we become complacent and stagnant.

The Bridges path takes this need for continual growth and deepening in faith and practice into account and provides a structure for the ongoing development of the faith community. In what follows, we highlight the steps on the path, and share with you the ways in which Catholic Life and Faith is ready to help you, as your partners in ministry.

THE BRIDGES PATH

Form servant leaders as bridge builders who:

Step One: Hold a common vision of the engaging and evangelizing community and who grasp the importance of building bridges to others within the community and beyond it;

Step Two: Deepen community by clarifying expectations and establishing a parish covenant through which parishioners are engaged as people who worship, connect, grow and serve;

Step Three: Build talents into strengths, develop strengths based ministry teams, and create a parish climate in which every person has the opportunity to contribute his or her best within the community;

Step Four: Lead and participate in guiding groups that carry the vision of an engaging and evangelizing community forward. These teams provide on-going input for initiatives in the four key areas of parish life (worship, connect, grow and serve) and take responsibility for building and strengthening bridges among parishioners through their area of influence and responsibility.

THE BRIDGES PATH

Develop a common vision of and begin to build the engaging and evangelizing community
Form your leaders (see resource list below)

Then:
Form four guiding teams

Worship	Connect	Grow	Serve
Mass, Sacraments, Liturgical Ministry Formation	Communal life, Welcome, Friendship	Call to Discipleship, Faith Formation for All	Call to Live as Stewards, Sharing of Self, Resources, Faith
Take stock of current of liturgical and sacramental practices	Take stock of current communal practices	Take stock of current discipleship and faith formation practices	Take stock of current stewardship, service, and outreach practices
Develop a plan to enhance the celebration of the liturgy and the ways people are formed for full, conscious and active participation	Develop and implement a parish covenant Enhance welcoming Create opportunities for friendship Connect team coordinates on-going development of community	Develop a comprehensive plan for faith formation-for-all 6 tasks of catechesis One size does not fit all	Develop a plan to form people as good stewards Strengths for individuals, in ministry teams; Strengths-based approach permeates parish Regular call to service, justice, mercy, ministry
On-going development via Worship team	On-going development via Connect team	On-going development via Grow team	On-going development via Serve team

Quarterly meeting of leaders
Annual retreat and renewal for leaders and for all
Skill development for servant leaders

HOW CATHOLIC LIFE AND FAITH IS READY TO PARTNER WITH YOU

Live and Virtual Events
Workbooks with Learning Videos and Guides
Parish Consulting and Partnership

The Bridges Series Servant Leader Formation:
The Engaging and Evangelizing Community
Developing a Positive Parish Leadership Structure
Creating a Culture of Strengths in the Parish
Strengths Based Ministry Teams
Skill Development for Servant Leaders

Bridges Resources for Guiding Groups:

Worship	Connect	Grow	Serve
Forming your Worship team	Forming your Connect (communal life) team	Forming your Grow (faith formation) team	Forming your Serve (stewardship and outreach) team
Taking Stock of Parish Worship and Liturgical Formation	Taking Stock of Parish Community Life	Taking Stock of Parish Discipleship Faith Formation	Taking Stock of Parish Stewardship and Outreach
Putting First Things First: The Liturgy as Operating Principle for Parish Life	Creating and Implementing a Parish Covenant Making Your Parish a Welcoming Place Person-to-Person: Inviting People to Become Friends	Come One, Come All: Comprehensive Faith Formation Ideas and Planning Engaging and Partnering with Parents A Summer Catechetical Option	Engaging People as Disciples and Stewards The Gifted Journey Discerning and Living our Call as Disciples

LEARNING VIDEOS AND GUIDES

The accompanying learning videos and guides are found here:

www.Bridge2Faith.net/module-1-materials

Your password is Bridges1 (password is cap sensitive)

The materials include:

1. Preparatory discussion guide

2. Learning videos which present content and will guide your discussions

3. A participant guide that accompanies the video

4. A post-session worksheet

5. An optional introduction to engagement video

Made in the USA
Middletown, DE
26 June 2015